Active Citizenship in Democracy

Rebecca Sjonger

CRABTREE
PUBLISHING COMPANY
WWW.CRABTREEBOOKS.COM

CRABTREE PUBLISHING COMPANY
WWW.CRABTREEBOOKS.COM

Author: Rebecca Sjonger
Series research and development:
 Janine Deschenes
Editors: Ellen Rodger, Janine Deschenes
Proofreader: Wendy Scavuzzo
Design and photo research: Katherine Berti
Print and production coordinator:
 Katherine Berti

Dedicated by Rebecca Sjonger:
For Lara, Sierra, and Talon
of the amazing Andersons

Front cover: In democracies, protesting is an essential right and one of the ways citizens make their views known to governments. These protesters gathered in Washington, D.C. to push for action on climate change.

Image credits:
Alamy Stock Photo
    Michael Wheatley: p. 42
    PA Images: p. 13 (bottom)
    Reuters: p. 40
    SOPA Images Limited: front cover
Flickr
    Anthony Quintano: p. 32
    Cory Doctorow: p. 38 (top)
Library of Congress: Leffler, Warren K., photographer: p. 14
Shutterstock
    Anton Garin: p. 30 (top inset)
    askarim: p. 28
    Brandon J Hale: p. 38 (bottom)
    Carol LeBlanc: p. 33 (bottom right)
    Chris Allan: p. 41 (bottom)
    Crush Rush: p. 35
    Daniel Avram: p. 9
    grandbrothers: p. 11 (top left)
    GTS Productions: p. 25 (bottom)
    Harry Thomas Flower: p. 29
    Hayk_Shalunts: p. 6 (bottom) hkalkan: p. 1
    ID stock photography: p. 12
    Ink Drop: p. 4
    Jamie Lamor Thompson: p. 34 (top right)
    Jana Asenbrennerova: p. 30 (bottom)
    Jelani Photography: p. 11 (bottom)
    Johnny Silvercloud: p. 33 (bottom left), 35 (bottom)
    Joseph Sohm: p. 24 (center right)
    Lawrey: p. 31 (top)
    Lev Radin: p. 18–19
    Liv Oeian: p. 27
    Lukas Maverick Greyson: p. 6 (top)
    Luigi Morris: p. 45
    Matt Gush: p. 21
    PaulWong: p. 17
    Phil Pasquini: p. 43
    pio3: p. 24 (left)
    Rob Crandall: p. 10
    R.M. Nunes: p. 16
    Sattalat Phukkum: p. 31 (bottom right)
    Shawn Goldberg: p. 36
    Simone Hogan: p. 20
    stock_photo_world: p. 23
    Trong Nguyen: p. 7 (bottom right)
Wikimedia Commons
    總統府: p. 17 (top)
    Leffler, Warren K., photographer: p. 13 (top)
    National Army Museum: p. 15 (bottom)
    vgGv1tsB1URdhg at Google Cultural Institute: p. 15 (top)
    www.trc.ca/assets/pdf/Volume_1_History_Part_1_English_Web.pdf: p. 41 (top)
www.youthrights.org—Screen Shot 2021-12-02 at 2.02.51 PM: p. 39 (inset)
All other images from Shutterstock

Crabtree Publishing Company
www.crabtreebooks.com   1-800-387-7650
Copyright © 2023 CRABTREE PUBLISHING COMPANY

All rights reserved. No part of this publication may be reproduced, stored in a retrieval system or be transmitted in any form or by any means, electronic, mechanical, photocopying, recording, or otherwise, without the prior written permission of Crabtree Publishing Company. In Canada: We acknowledge the financial support of the Government of Canada through the Canada Book Fund for our publishing activities.

Printed in the U.S.A./072022/CG20220201

Published in Canada
Crabtree Publishing
616 Welland Ave.
St. Catharines, Ontario
L2M 5V6

Published in the United States
Crabtree Publishing
347 Fifth Ave
Suite 1402-145
New York, NY 10016

Library and Archives Canada Cataloguing in Publication
Available at the Library and Archives Canada
Library of Congress Cataloging-in-Publication Data
Available at the Library of Congress

Hardcover: 9781039663305   Paperback: 9781039663794
Ebook (pdf): 9781039668225   Epub: 9781039685628
Read-along: 9781039686113   Audio book: 9781039668713

Contents

INTRODUCTION 4

CHAPTER 1
Features and Flaws 8

CHAPTER 2
Everyone Plays a Part 20

CHAPTER 3
Responsible Democracy 28

CHAPTER 4
Strengthening Democracy 36

WRAP UP
Active Citizenship 42

Learn More 44

BIBLIOGRAPHY 46

GLOSSARY 47

INDEX 48

About the Author 48

Introduction

You may not be able to vote yet, but you can use the rights protected in democracy to make change.

Young people all over the world are doing it—whether through anti-racist **protests**, taking part in model governments, or joining global climate strikes. Youth are strengthening democracy by exercising one of the fundamental democratic rights: participation. By participating, they are learning how democracies work and developing solutions to the problems that threaten democracy. The word "democracy" describes a kind of government. It also describes a process of rule by and for the "demos," the Greek word for people. Some democracies are large, such as the ones that run cities, states, provinces or territories, and countries. They can also be small, such as student governments at your school. In most democracies today, people vote to choose who will speak and act for them. These are called representative democracies. The elected leaders represent the voters. Keep reading to find out what healthy democracies look like and the many ways to keep them that way.

Climate change is one issue in which young people have become experts at protesting.

Canada's parliament is where laws are developed, discussed, and passed.

Democratic Processes

Processes are steps taken to meet certain goals. Some of them are linked to democracy. These processes engage citizens in important duties such as voting and serving on **juries**. (Find out more about these responsibilities in Chapter 2.) They allow democratic governments and other groups to function. Processes can also help people make fair decisions. At the start of the **deliberative process**, for example, an idea is proposed. A group considers and evaluates it. Then they decide which action to take. They could vote on it as well. The **majority** of people hold the power in democracies. The successful proposal or **candidate** is the one with greatest number of supporters.

Democratic Ideals

Values and principles are important to democracy, too. Democratic governments and processes must be fair and accountable. People should be treated equally. That means they all have the same opportunities. This human right is at the heart of democracy. Human rights are the basic freedoms and privileges that every person is born with. Strong democracies uphold these rights. For example, citizens are protected against discrimination. This occurs when groups or individuals are treated badly because of things such as their race, gender, age, or disability. In a democratic society, everyone is free to make their own choices. They are expected to work together for the common good, however. This book describes fights for democracy and how you can uphold democratic values.

Democracy in Action

A Death Sparks a Movement

In February 2012, Trayvon Martin was visiting a home in a **gated community** in Florida. The 17-year-old Black youth went out to get candy and iced tea. As he walked back from the store, George Zimmerman spotted him. Zimmerman was on patrol with the neighborhood anti-crime group and carried a gun. He stopped Trayvon because he thought he looked suspicious. There was a struggle, then Zimmerman shot and killed Trayvon. Zimmerman claimed that he was defending himself and was not immediately charged. After months of investigation, in April 2012, a special prosecutor appointed by Florida's governor charged Zimmerman with second-degree murder. At trial, Zimmerman was found not guilty for Trayvon's death. The case led to weeks of nationwide demonstrations. Many people believed that the police and justice system failed Trayvon. In 2013, Patrisse Cullors, Alicia Garza, and Opal Tometi formed the Black Lives Matter Network to end violence and discrimination against Black people. They spread the hashtag #blacklivesmatter through social media. The BLM movement continues to fight for democratic values such as equality and inclusion. Protests have been held around the world.

BLM also raises awareness of abuses of power. In some cases, this has led to action. When George Floyd was killed by Minneapolis police in 2020, democratic protests led to President Biden calling for an investigation. The officer who killed Floyd was convicted of murder.

Defining Democracy

A list of common terms

Citizen A person who is legally recognized to have the privileges of those who were born in or live in a particular place

Constitution The foundational laws that guide a country

Election A vote in which someone is chosen to hold a certain position

Political Relating to jobs and actions that have control over how a country or group runs

Political party A group of people who work together to get likeminded candidates elected

Representative democracy A government that is chosen by citizens who vote for leaders to represent them

System Parts that work together to meet a common purpose

CHAPTER 1
Features and Flaws

There are almost 200 countries around the world. Each one has its own values, processes, and government. Fewer than half of them are democratic.

Full democracies do their best to uphold democratic principles and systems. This does not happen on its own—a lot of effort goes into keeping a democracy healthy. Individuals and communities must work together to solve problems as they arise. Government leaders take responsibility, too. There are several reports and **indexes** that rank democracies throughout the world. These are put together by organizations concerned about democracy. Researchers for the Economist Group, a for-profit media group, rank democracy levels around the world each year. In 2020, the Economist Group democracy index ranked about 12 countries as full democracies. The same index showed about 4 out of 10 people in the world live in flawed democracies. They face one or more challenges, which are described in the rest of this chapter.

8

Rights and Freedoms

People who live in democracies expect their rights to be respected. These places usually have written lists of their citizens' rights. The United States has the Bill of Rights, for example. Canada has the Canadian Charter of Rights and Freedoms. These documents do more than protect people. They also help to shape society. Liberty is highly valued in democracies. This is the state of being free, in which citizens are able to control their own lives. They choose their government leaders. They can also live wherever they want. Traveling around as well as in and out of their country is allowed. People can decide which kind of job to work at. They may also own businesses and property. Everyone can share their opinions freely, and citizens can meet with whomever they want. In democracies, rights and responsibilities, or duties, go together. Rights are given and responsibilities are followed. Democracies require public participation from the people who live in them. One way individuals do this is by becoming informed and involved. Voting is a way people in democracies have their say. There are many other ways democracies are strengthened.

Check It Out!

U.S. Bill of Rights:

www.archives.gov/founding-docs/bill-of-rights-transcript

Canadian Charter of Rights and Freedoms:

https://laws-lois.justice.gc.ca/eng/const/page-12.html

Democracies allow freedom of movement—unless there is some sort of emergency or threat. Then, some freedoms might be temporarily restricted. Individual rights are always tempered with the rights of the whole.

Busy voting stations, like this one in Virginia, show how citizens engage in elections.

Ballot Blues

Government leaders answer to voters. Citizens can re-elect **politicians** or choose new people to represent them. Democracy is weakened when people are not informed, lose interest, or stop taking part. Voter apathy, or lack of interest, is a major issue, for example. This occurs when individuals feel that their votes do not matter, so they do not bother participating. This leads to low voter turnout. Then the elected leaders are chosen by a smaller number of citizens. They may not reflect the views of the majority of people. Becoming involved in the political process by learning about political ideas and parties is one way to combat apathy. When people see that that their ideas and actions are taken seriously and can make a difference, they are more likely to continue voting and supporting democracy. Voter **suppression** is another serious problem. This occurs when certain groups are actively discouraged from voting. Learn more about it on page 33.

Free and Fair Elections

Elections take place regularly in democracies. For example, Canadian national elections are held once every four years. The ruling political party will often call an election when it is popular with voters. This increases the party's chance of winning. Other parties can also force an election, when the majority of representatives must get together to vote that they have no confidence in the government. This makes leaders accountable for their actions. American presidential elections take place on the first or second Tuesday in November every four years. In 2020, the voting process in the United States faced serious issues. The results were questioned by many in the losing Republican party. They argued that ballots were not valid for a variety of reasons. Strong democracies have processes by which citizens can question the results of an election and where investigations can be made.

There should always be room for dissent, or opinions that differ from those of others. But opinions should be based on facts instead of just partisanship, or the strong support of a party or cause.

Encouraging civic engagement strengthens democracy. This includes volunteering and learning about issues important to people and communities. For young people, model governments and youth parliaments help them learn about democratic processes.

Working Together

Political tolerance, or being open to other points of view, is a central democratic virtue. Everyone is encouraged to share their point of view in a democracy. Opposing perspectives should be considered with respect. That does not mean ideas that are harmful have to be accepted without question. Democracy is threatened when citizens and leaders put getting their own way ahead of being openminded. The majority rules in a democracy. However, smaller numbers of people who have different opinions should have the same rights. Democratic governments must take the views of these **minority** groups into account. Flawed democracies often have problems with political tolerance and how they treat people who are in the minority.

Case Study

Blocking with Filibusters

Government leaders use the deliberative process when they make laws or other proposals. This usually includes multiple stages of a bill or motion being read, debated, and revised. Sometimes, one or more leaders do not want to see something succeed. They stall so there is not enough time to vote on it. This is called a filibuster. The rules for how it is carried out vary from place to place. Filibusters put democracy in danger by forcing a certain result. They may block one political party's plans for another party's benefit. They can also be used to protect people in authority. For example, in 2020, a motion was proposed to investigate how much was paid to members of Canadian prime minister Justin Trudeau's family members to speak at a charity event held by an organization in line for government contracts. Government members from the Liberal Party, of which Trudeau is the head, filibustered the motion to keep the leader's information from being shared publicly. In the United States, Senator Strom Thurmond holds the record for longest filibuster. He spoke for more than 24 hours in the hopes of preventing the **Civil Rights Act** from passing in 1957. His tactics failed.

Strom Thurmond

Canadian Liberal Party members of parliament used a filibuster to block a motion to investigate the prime minister's family connections to the WE charity. Here, the prime minister's wife speaks at a WE event.

A number of Civil Rights acts passed from 1957 through the 1960s were intended to prohibit discrimination in voting practices, public places, and housing. Still, rights could be denied and people had to press governments to enforce laws. Here, African Americans demand their rights as citizens in front of the White House in 1965.

Legal Rights

Another core democratic value is the rule of law. This means that all citizens are treated equally. No one is above the law, including police officers and political leaders. Democracy is weakened when people in authority abuse it. Basic human rights are also in danger. The Black Lives Matter movement shows what happens when citizens refuse to allow inequality and injustice. Leaders must be held accountable for their actions. To help prevent the misuse of power, no one person or group is given total control. Instead, roles and responsibilities must be shared. Find out more about how this works in the next chapter.

Think About It!

Based on what you have read so far, how healthy do you think democracy is in your own community or country?

Democracy at Risk

The United States has long been viewed as a leading example of western, or **liberal democracy**. In the 1700s, some British colonists living in North America resented their lack of representation in the British government. Thirteen colonies—the United States—approved the Declaration of Independence on July 4, 1776. It emphasized the rights of individuals. It also included the right to revolt against the tyranny of a **monarch**. Britain recognized the new country's independence at the end of the American Revolution. The U.S. Constitution came into effect in 1789. A constitution lays out the fundamental laws of a nation.

King George III ruled the American colonies from across the Atlantic Ocean in the 1700s.

The United States won its revolutionary war against Britain in 1783.

Flawed Democracies

Over the following centuries, many developing democracies borrowed from the U.S. Constitution. They also used the American system of government. However, the United States has been ranked as a flawed democracy since 2017. This shows that even the most vibrant democracies can falter and that democracy needs constant re-enforcement. Some of the problems that need to be addressed include the country's voting system and how its political parties work together. Organizations such as Freedom House, a non-profit research organization in Washington, D.C., believe strengthening public support for democratic values and principals would help. This means educating people on the importance of independent courts, human rights, and a free press.

Failed Democracies

When a democracy fails, it may be the result of a leader staying in power unopposed. This can lead to an autocracy. Unlike a democracy, one person or a small group of leaders controls this kind of government. They use their power to defeat whoever opposes them. In the 1980s, for example, many Latin American countries were democracies. As corrupt leaders took power, they often became flawed or failed democracies. The only full democracies left in the region are Chile, Costa Rica, and Uruguay.

Check It Out!

The United States Constitution is the world's oldest written constitution.

www.archives.gov/founding-docs/constitution-transcript

Chile emerged as a democracy in 1990, after the 17-year dictatorship of Augusto Pinochet. Chileans demanded a new constitution in 2019, and a referendum held in 2021 resulted in a favorable vote. The previous constitution was written by an advisor to Pinochet and gave elites and the police more power in Chilean society. A new constitution is just one more step toward a stronger democracy in Chile.

Democracies in Name Only

Some countries claim to be democratic; however, their leaders do not represent their citizens. The Democratic Republic of the Congo, for example, is actually an autocracy. Elections are held there but the results are usually rigged. Steps toward democracy have been slowed by conflicts in the region. People who live in autocracies do not have the same freedoms as citizens of democracies. However, many are fighting for their rights. They can be supported by protestors and democratic governments.

Eswatini, a country in southern Africa, is an example of an absolute monarchy. Royal rulers, such as King Mswati III, hold more power. They can choose government leaders. This makes this a form of autocracy.

Students have been prominent in pro-democracy demonstrations in Hong Kong. The umbrellas prevent the government's facial recognition systems and cameras from identifying protestors' faces.

Attack on the Capitol

On January 6, 2021, thousands of Americans who believed the 2020 presidential election was stolen from Donald Trump tried to overturn the election results and stop Joe Biden from becoming the new president. The event has become known as the 2021 Capitol Attack. The protestors and attackers gathered at the United States Capitol and disrupted Congress during the count of Electoral College ballots. This is the last stage in confirming a president. An estimated 800 people managed to enter the Capitol building. Five people died and 138 were injured. Months later, a special committee of Congress investigated the attack and called on people involved to testify and give more information. Some were indicted, or charged, with contempt of Congress for refusing to cooperate.

Think About It!

After a mob overtook the U.S. Capitol in 2021, Somali-American Congresswoman Ilhan Omar said, "I never expected to experience a direct assault on democracy in the United States, one of the oldest, most prosperous democracies in the world." What does this reveal about the need to protect democracy?

CHAPTER 2
Everyone Plays a Part

Individuals must work together for a democracy to function well. Everyone is expected to take part. Roles include voters, government representatives, the public service, taxpayers, jurors, and protestors. They all contribute to keeping a democratic society thriving.

Voters

Voting is both a right and a responsibility in democracies. The age at which people can vote in an election depends on the place. In the United States and Canada, citizens can vote after they turn 18 years old. They may elect leaders ranging from the mayor of a town to the president or prime minister of a country. Voters could also decide who will lead other groups. For example, your local school board may be made up of elected members. They represent their community's interests. Young people can take part in this democratic process through student governments. All voters must learn about the candidates and their goals. This helps them decide who they want to speak and act on their behalf. They must be allowed to make their selections without any outside pressure. Political parties can ask people to vote for them. They cannot enforce it in a democracy, however. Voters are given privacy so they can make their choices freely.

Balancing civil liberties, or freedoms, with public health and safety proved to be a challenge to democracies during the COVID-19 pandemic 2020–2022. Governments made restrictions on freedom of movement. They balanced those with the right to security of the person. Most citizens in democracies supported temporary limits on freedoms for the good of all.

Being Informed

Voters hold power over their elected representatives in a democracy. Citizens are able to show their approval or disapproval in each election. This means that they must stay well informed. They need to know whether they are being represented properly. Then they can decide whether they support their leaders' actions. Staying up to date on important issues that affect them also prepares them to vote in referendums. These are regional or national votes that pose a single question to voters. Referendums help settle major disputes in a fair manner. If citizens are **indifferent** to what their governments are doing, leaders become less accountable for what they say and do. This makes it easier for them to abuse their power.

Think About It!

Do you think voters should choose leaders who represent them personally, or who represent the greater good for all citizens? Why?

Running for Office

Most adults have the right to run as political candidates in the United States and Canada. Historically, governments in these countries have been made up of people who are male, White, and wealthy. They have dominated the executive branches in particular. In 2021, the newly elected U.S. Congress was the most diverse group ever. Even so, fewer than one-quarter of the representatives were from non-White backgrounds. Democracies must address unequal representation. Citizens from all backgrounds should be well represented in governments.

Government Representatives

In the United States and Canada, government representatives are found at three levels. They are part of the municipal, state or provincial/territorial, and federal governments. Municipal, or local, leaders run cities and smaller places. They are often grouped together into counties, districts, or regions. These areas may have their own government bodies. Mayors often lead at the local level. They work alongside a group of councillors. This level runs parks, libraries, police forces, and other community services. At the state or provincial/territorial level, there is another assembly of elected representatives. They are led by state governors or provincial/terriorial premiers. This middle level has more authority than local leaders. They control major areas such as health care and education. National leaders oversee things that affect an entire country. A president or prime minister oversees this level. They work with a small group of department leaders. There is a larger group of elected representatives, as well. Politicians at every level serve the people who voted for them—as well as those who did not.

The chart below shows racial/ethnic diversity in the 117th U.S. Congress.

- ● African-American
- ● Hispanic
- ○ White
- ● Asian/Pacific Islander
- ● Indigenous

House—439 seats

REPUBLICANS   DEMOCRATS

Senate—100 seats

REPUBLICANS   DEMOCRATS

Limited Power

The powers of democratic governments are limited by the constitution of the country. They have enough authority to do their duties. They cannot abuse it for their own gain, though. Checks and balances limit power by spreading it to three branches: executive, legislative, and judiciary. In the United States, for example, the legislative branch can introduce draft bills, but the executive branch led by the president cannot. The lawmakers need the president to approve their bills, though. The president could also veto, or reject, bills. This makes the president very powerful. Term limits help prevent a leader from gaining too much control over time. The American president can only serve for two four-year periods. Canadian prime ministers do not have fixed terms. However, they and their government, can be thrown out of power if the majority of representatives vote against them. If any representative does not uphold democratic values, they risk losing the next election.

Government Level	Executive Branch	Legislative Branch	Judicial Branch
	Highest authority in a government; includes a small group of department leaders	Elected leaders who work together to make laws	Elected and appointed judges who interpret laws made by the other branches and oversee court systems
Federal	President/ Prime Minister	Member of Congress/ Member of Parliament	Supreme Court Justices
State/Provincial/ Territorial	Governor/Premier	Legislative Representatives	State/Provincial/ Territorial Judges
Municipal	Mayor	Councillors	Municipal Judges

A voter speaks to city politicians during a public hearing on an issue in Austin, Texas. Public meetings are one way voters can express their opinions directly to their elected representatives.

Public Service

Each level and branch of a democratic government employs people who are not elected representatives. Instead, they are part of the public service, sometimes called the civil service. This group supports government and keeps many government **institutions** and services running. They answer to government, not to political parties. They hold a huge range of jobs, from teachers to postal carriers. Other members of the public service help carry out processes within government departments. They usually keep their positions as the politicians they work alongside are voted in and out. This is an important group in a democracy. Depending on their roles, public servants may advise politicians and help them make decisions. They are the experts on how government works. This makes them just as accountable to citizens as elected leaders are. A variety of departments enact a country's laws and uphold its standards. If they do not respect fairness and human rights, it affects citizens' everyday lives.

Taxpayers

Paying taxes is an essential democratic process. The government collects money, which it uses to fund its systems and services. When someone is paid for working, for instance, a percentage of their income goes to the government. The Internal Revenue Service (IRS) collects income taxes in the United States. The Canada Revenue Agency (CRA) collects it from Canadians.

Income taxes are direct taxes as they are paid by a taxpayer directly to the government. Similar agencies collect taxes in other democracies. Businesses also pay a variety of taxes. People of all ages pay sales taxes. This is a set percentage that is added to the sale of many goods and services. Sales taxes are indirect taxes. They are paid to merchants who then pass them on to the government. The amount varies by location.

Property owners pay taxes to their municipal governments. This helps pay for local community services. People who earn less money usually pay lower income taxes—but they pay the same indirect taxes on goods and services. Sometimes, people and companies find ways to avoid paying taxes and leave the burden for others to carry. Candidates for election may promise to lower taxes. This is often popular with voters. However, if there are not enough funds to cover government expenses, services may be cut.

Most goods sold in the United States and Canada are taxed.

In democracies, taxpayers contribute to the common good. Taxes are used to build roads, pay for social security, Medicare or health care, and defense and security, among other things.

Jury Duty

People who are charged with a crime have the right to be judged by a jury of their peers. Most citizens are expected to serve on juries when needed. It is a **civic duty**. In the United States and Canada, jury duty is mandatory and people summoned or called for jury duty must attend. Jurors are randomly chosen from a pool of eligible people who are over the age of 18. Usually, they have no legal knowledge. They are expected to be **impartial** as they examine the evidence. Then they must agree on a ruling. Being open to other people's perspectives is an important democratic principle. Keeping an open mind is necessary as a juror. If they discriminate or are unjust in any way, it is unfair. While jury duty is a common part of most democracies, a few countries such as Malaysia have banned it. They believe it has too much potential for unfairness.

In the United States and Canada, people who have a conscientious objection can be excused from jury duty. These are usually people whose personal or religious beliefs prevent them from making judgements on punishments.

Protestors and Petitioners

People who live in democracies consent, or agree, to be governed. They also agree to follow the rule of law and uphold the public good. This does not mean they give up their freedoms. It means governments get their powers from the people. In liberal democracies, citizens are welcome to protest and petition, for example. Protests allow people to use their democratic freedom of speech. They also have the freedom to assemble. This helps them gain attention and raise awareness. Protests show representatives how many citizens care about an issue. In Colombia, for instance, a massive protest against proposed tax increases took place in 2021. Protestors may also bring attention to global issues. Swedish **activist** Greta Thunberg sparked the School Strikes for Climate protests. They spread around the world, including the United States and Canada. Petitions, on the other hand, appeal for change in writing. Petitioners collect the signatures of citizens who agree with the proposal. Leaders are able to see exactly what the people they represent want from them. Protestors and petitioners strengthen a democracy by allowing citizens to take part and make changes. If people ignore problems or wait for someone else to act, democracy is at risk.

Think About It!

Have you ever taken part in a protest or signed a petition? What moved you to act?

Climate activist Greta Thunberg led students in Sweden on regular Friday climate protests. Most were not old enough to vote, but their opinions still counted. The School Strikes for Climate protests caught the attention of media and some leaders.

CHAPTER 3
Responsible Democracy

People all have their own interests and goals. Sometimes, these connect with their roles in a democracy.

Voters choose representatives who will make decisions that benefit them. Members of government and the public service would like to hold onto their jobs. Taxpayers want to keep as much of their money as they can, and also get the services that are important to them. Citizens may also belong to special interest groups, the media, and political parties.

Special Interest Groups

Civil society describes organizations that are not governments or businesses. There is a wide range of these networks of people. They include faith-based groups, community services, environmental activists, and **unions**. Much like a government, they represent the interests of their members. Citizens that form these groups often share common goals, and they work together to achieve them. They may focus on anything from human rights to gun control. They raise awareness in many ways. For example, they can protest, run promotional programs, or **lobby** the government.

Large corporations lobby government, as well. They want to ensure that their interests are considered when governments make laws and regulations. This isn't necessarily bad, but can cause problems when their interests are given more weight than citizens'.

28

American Senator Ted Cruz meets with voters outside a National Rifle Association meeting in Texas. Interest groups also play a role in democracies. They can ensure that the voices and interests of a wide range of citizens are heard.

Potential Conflicts

Lobbyists try to sway elected representatives at all levels. They may try to influence members of the public service, too. Their job is to get help meeting their groups' goals. This can be done through changing rules or laws, or by getting government funding. A special interest group may convince a leader to make a decision that is not in the best interests of all citizens. When politicians are too closely linked with these groups, they may place more value on the interest group's goals than those of ordinary citizens. That means they have two opposing goals and cannot represent citizens in the way that they should. This can be a threat to democracy.

Think About It!

Do you think special interest groups make a democracy stronger or weaker? Why?

29

Media and Democracy

Members of the media research, report on, and spread news stories. They help to inform citizens. In a democracy, journalists are free to investigate and describe the government's actions. People often believe what they read in newspapers or hear on news broadcasts. This gives the media a lot of power. They must avoid putting their own personal interests ahead of the public good when relaying stories. Some media outlets, such as newspapers or television stations, have a bias. This is unfair treatment for or against a thing, person, or group. They could also have their own goals, which might be hidden from others. This may interfere with journalists' ability to share the facts. They may even be forced to take a certain angle on a story. Some media sources are open about their interests. Most people are aware of their biases. For example, a conservative American news station is likely to report favorably about Republicans, while a liberal news station might criticize them.

Citizens must think critically about what to believe. Looking at multiple news sources is helpful.

In democracies, the media acts to hold government accountable for its actions. This includes asking politicians questions and informing the public.

Democracies allow for a diverse range of opinions and media from a number of different sources. This allows more freedom of speech.

Freedom of Speech

When freedom of speech is blocked, democratic values are threatened. The same is true for the freedom of the press. If a government **censors** or tries to control the media, it abuses its power. This is common in autocracies. Seeing it in a democracy is a warning sign of a serious flaw. Free speech also means that anyone can post to social media. It spreads facts and misinformation faster and more widely than ever before. It is easy for citizens to share their views widely. No one has to wait for reporting from traditional media. This helps the fight for democracy and puts it at risk at the same time.

Some media sources encourage outrage because they make it easy to make statements that cannot easily be checked for accuracy.

Think About It!

How does the media exploring multiple points of view help make a democracy stronger?

Political Parties

Members of political parties share similar goals for what they want their government leaders to do on their behalf. They work together to help people from their party get elected. This increases their representation in government. Anyone can form a political party that reflects their beliefs and interests. Most candidates who are up for election belong to political parties. They get help with their campaigns from their party. Voters have a good idea about which issues are important to candidates based on which party they belong to. Some focus on the environment, whereas others promote business ventures. Parties may have divisions that are especially for young people. Youth can also get involved in campaigns.

Having a number of different political parties allows voters to choose between competing ideas.

Democratic Voting

In democracies, voters must be able to choose from at least two political parties in national elections. The Democrats and Republicans are the main parties in the United States. Most of the power is held by the Liberal and Conservative parties in the Canadian government. In both countries, these parties appeal to distinct groups of voters. There is a risk of them looking out for their own best interests instead of the common good of all. Political tolerance means people with opposing perspectives can still work together. Democracy is threatened when people from different parties are unable to listen to and consider one another's views. Another major concern is the fight for power. It can be more important to a party to control the government than to serve citizens. One way to take control is voter suppression. Some citizens are targeted because one party believes they will support an opponent. Suppression tactics include unfair rules about identification or early voting. This makes it difficult for people to cast their ballots. Citizens must fight problems like voter suppression by staying informed and spreading awareness. They can also demand change from their representatives.

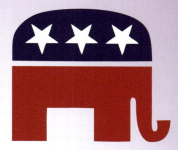

The Republican Party is also known as the GOP ("Grand Old Party").

DNC stands for Democratic National Committee.

Elections were difficult during the 2020–2022 COVID-19 pandemic. Many democratic countries explored more options for allowing people to vote. These included more mail-in voting ballots and extended polling hours.

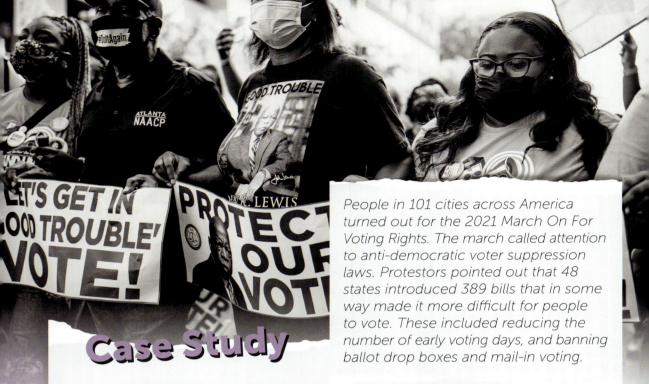

People in 101 cities across America turned out for the 2021 March On For Voting Rights. The march called attention to anti-democratic voter suppression laws. Protestors pointed out that 48 states introduced 389 bills that in some way made it more difficult for people to vote. These included reducing the number of early voting days, and banning ballot drop boxes and mail-in voting.

Case Study

Georgia 2020

Democrat Stacey Abrams ran to be governor of Georgia in 2018. She came close to winning. This surprised some people because the state traditionally voted for Republicans. Abrams is an **advocate** for voting rights. After losing the race for governor, she turned her attention to the 2020 presidential election. She led a group of activists to promote voting to minority groups. They also improved ballot access for people who had been blocked by registration and identification rules. Her overall goal was to flip the state to the Democrats. However, Abrams claimed that "the message is not trying to persuade them to share Democratic values. Your message is to persuade them that voting can actually yield change." She helped the Democrats win in 2020. Afterward, state leaders in Georgia changed their voting laws. For example, they made it more difficult to vote early or use drop boxes, both of which Black voters relied on.

Stacey Abrams was the first Black woman to run for governor of Georgia.

Democratic Duties

Upholding democracy is everyone's responsibility. Special interest groups, the media, and political parties should all practice democratic values while achieving their goals. If you live in a democracy, it is your responsibility, too! What does this look like?

- Finding out who benefits from a group's actions.
- Watching for conflicts of interest and pointing them out if they happen.
- Becoming well informed before taking a side on political issues.
- Being openminded with people who have opposing views.
- Asking whether one group's rights and freedoms are hurting another group.
- Challenging people to better understand what a democracy stands for.

CHAPTER 4
Strengthening Democracy

People of all ages can take part in, improve, and protect democracy. A society that defends democratic values will have a strong democratic government and processes.

Exploring how these principles are practiced in your community and your country is a great way to get started. Find out how healthy democracy is in each level of your government. Research which constitutional rights you have as a citizen. Democracies are strongly linked to human rights. The United Nations lists 30 of them in its Universal Declaration of Human Rights. Familiarize yourself with these rights (see link in box on the right). Consider how they affect you and your fellow citizens.

Check It Out!

United Nations Universal Declaration of Human Rights:

www.un.org/en/udhrbook/pdf/udhr_booklet_en_web.pdf

Democracies are always evolving and should work to correct wrongs of the past and present. These people are acknowledging that the land they live on is Indigenous territory. It is one step toward becoming more inclusive, fair, and democratic.

Think About It!

How do laws and rules help people resolve conflicts fairly and peacefully?

Investigate Your Democracy

Democracies protect their citizens' liberty. Remember, everyone is free to make their own choices. But, if people only do what is in their own best interests, the common good may be ignored. You can see this at work in your home or at school. Note how people use their freedoms. Do they help or hurt others? Which decisions help the greatest number of people? Which actions seem self-centered? This can be applied to your wider community, as well. Fairness is another important democratic principle. That is why laws are in place to protect the people who are in the minority. The rule of law is also crucial in a democracy. Citizens are expected to obey laws because they chose the representatives who made them. Study the rules that you must follow in your classroom. What purposes do they serve? Note any unfairness or inequalities. Remember that political tolerance is a key democratic virtue. Pay attention to how different political parties are described by people you know or in the news. Respectfully point out biases when you notice them. Encourage others to be openminded, too!

Accountability

Democratic principles can also be used to tackle issues in society. For example, accountability keeps democracies healthy. The media, members of the public service, and voters can hold government leaders responsible for what they say and do. "Watchdogs" are groups that guard against wrongdoing. Sometimes, these are departments within a government. In Canada, for instance, the Privacy Commissioner inspects how well the government protects citizens' privacy. The Canadian Auditor General monitors government spending. American government watchdogs include the Government Accountability Office. It looks at how taxes are spent among other things. Watchdogs put out reports for the public to see. Law enforcement officers are also accountable for their actions. Internal Affairs divisions monitor the police to prevent the misuse of power. Citizens and private groups can also act as watchdogs.

Black Lives Matter protests in 2020, pushed for reforms and accountability in policing. Some studies have shown that police killings decreased in some cities where large and more frequent protests were held.

The U.S. Government Accountability Office is an agency that is known as a "Congressional watchdog." It helps ensure government money is spent well.

Participate in Processes

Processes are another way for people to get involved in democracy. When you pay for something that is taxed, you are financially supporting government services. Voting can also lead the way for positive changes. New leaders often mean new priorities. If you are too young to vote, you can still encourage others to do it! Upholding the rule of law can include being a juror or pointing out inequalities. This ensures fairness in court systems. Deliberative processes are another way to keep democracies strong. They are used in a wide variety of settings. Democratic decision-making also uses consensus, or aiming to get wide agreement. This requires discussion, valuing and considering other people's ideas, and being willing to change opinions.

Strengthening Democracies

When individuals and groups put their own interests aside and work together, they can strengthen a democracy. For example, citizens can be on the lookout for ways to improve fairness and equality in their own communities. You could do this at school. Start by listing ways that everyday routines could be made more accessible to the greatest number of students. For example, do you listen to daily announcements over a speaker? How could that leave out some people? Can someone who uses a wheelchair easily access every space? Which groups might be able to help improve any issues you find? Taking part in democracy often starts with being informed. Look at issues that affect people who are different from you. The media reports on problems that minority groups face. However, the majority must then pay attention and take responsibility to help others. This can be done through protesting, petitioning, and contacting government representatives.

Some groups have proposed lowering the voting age to 16. This was done for school board election in Oakland, California, in 2020.

39

Case Study

Residential Schools

In 2021, many non-Indigenous people around the world were shocked when news reported that experts using **ground-penetrating radar** located what is believed to be up to 200 unmarked graves of Indigenous children in Canada. The findings were made at the Kamloops **Residential School** in British Columbia. The investigation is still ongoing and there are plans to carefully dig the site for remains. Indigenous people had always known these sites existed. Many children were known to have died of illness, hunger, intentional harm, and accidents after being taken from their parents and sent to residential schools. Searches have found more of what are believed to be thousands of unmarked graves at other residential school sites across Canada.

From 1831 to 1996, the government funded more than 130 of these schools. Most were operated by Christian churches and religious organizations. They were designed to assimilate, or stamp out, Indigenous cultures. Over 150,000 children were torn from their families and sent to the schools. They were often badly mistreated. Canadians were **polled** after the news broke. Two-thirds said they knew little about the residential school system. Indigenous people had been pressing the government for years to help find the remains as part of a process of **reconciliation**. When the bodies were found, **settlers** finally began to listen to what Indigenous people had been saying for decades. Many recognized that everyone is responsible for knowing their country's history, then taking action in the present. They demanded that leaders address the issues that survivors and their families face.

Canadian Prime Minister Justin Trudeau places a teddy bear on a grave at the Cowessess First Nation in Saskatchewan. The site was part of a residential school where radar found what is believed to be 751 graves. The Cowessess First Nation is examining church records to identify each child buried there.

Children in residential schools were not allowed to speak their own languages or follow their cultures. The schools operated for more than 160 years. The last one closed in 1996.

Every Child Matters is the slogan of Orange Shirt Day. It is marked on September 30 to commemorate the suffering of children in residential schools. At age 6, Phyllis (Jack) Webstad wore a new orange shirt on her first day at residential school. The shirt was taken from her, as if she didn't matter.

Check It Out!

Canada's National Centre for Truth and Reconciliation is a resource for anyone who wants to help resolve injustices against Indigenous peoples.

https://nctr.ca

WRAP UP
Active Citizenship

Democracies can only be healthy and vibrant if citizens get involved. Voting and governing are major factors. However, there is a lot more to it!

Brigette DePape is a Canadian activist who worked as a Senate page. She launched a silent protest in the House of Commons in 2011 to protest government policies.

Younger people can take part by upholding democratic principles and processes. They can get informed and educate others. Solving problems together helps prevent democracies from becoming flawed or even failing. The future can be changed right now.

Get to Know Your Democracy

The previous chapter encouraged you to investigate democracy in your community and your country. Asking questions can help you get started:

- Which political parties are active in your community? Which issues are important to them? How well do they work together?

- Who are your elected leaders at the three different levels of government? How could you contact them?

- Are there groups in your school that uphold democratic principles? If not, could you start one?

- What could you do to promote democracy in your home, at school, and in your community?

Think About It!

Have you already been taking part in democracy somehow without realizing it? What have you been doing?

Take Action

Keep an open mind as you read news articles and opinion pieces. Look for biases and compare multiple sources. Highlight what your representatives at each level of government are saying and doing. Research how people in your community can get involved in elections. If there are debates or rallies being held locally, check them out. You could learn a lot about issues that affect you or your family. Keep democratic principles in mind, too. Study how tolerant people are of opposing views. Point out discrimination and inequality whenever you notice them. You can promote democratic values and encourage others to join you. Young people are the future—you can make a difference!

Indigenous land protectors call upon President Biden to declare a climate emergency in 2021.

Learn More

What stood out to you in this book? Do you want to learn more about human rights, supporting minority groups, the voting process, or student activism? Use the links below to dive in.

Part of understanding democracy is being aware of basic human rights. Review the U.N.'s Universal Declaration of Human Rights at:	www.un.org/en/udhrbook/pdf/udhr_booklet_en_web.pdf
The Anti-Defamation League provides helpful resources related to democratic values. For example, check out its tips for holding respectful conversations.	www.adl.org/education/resources/tools-and-strategies/can-we-talk-tips-for-respectful-conversations-in-schools
Ideas for young activists:	www.adl.org/education/resources/tools-and-strategies/10-ways-youth-can-engage-in-activism
Rock the Vote is an American organization that encourages democratic participation.	www.rockthevote.org
To learn about the elections process in the United States, visit:	www.usa.gov/election
For Canadian information, go to:	electionsanddemocracy.ca/canadas-elections
CBC Kids News has created a video and information page with everything you need to know about the Black Lives Matter movement.	www.cbc.ca/kidsnews/post/watch-what-canadian-kids-should-know-about-blacklivesmatter
The National Democratic Institute in Washington, D.C., has a website dedicated to youth participation.	https://changemycommunity.ctb.ku.edu
Human Rights Watch is an organization that defends rights all over the world. Check out their videos for teachers and students.	https://www.hrw.org/students-and-educators

Think About It!

Is there a human rights issue that affects your community or country? How could you use democratic principles to take action and help?

Bibliography

Introduction

Black Lives Matter. blacklivesmatter.com

"Citizenship Education Resources." CIVIX. civix.ca/resources

"Defining Democracy." Facing History & Ourselves. https://bit.ly/3p8qhxD

"Democracy." United Nations. www.un.org/en/global-issues democracy

Hauser, Christine, Derrick Bryson Taylor, and Neil Vigdor. "'I Can't Breathe': 4 Minneapolis Officers Fired After Black Man Dies in Custody." *The New York Times*, May 26, 2020. https://nyti.ms/32yJwsy

Heslop, D. Alan. "political system." *Britannica*. https://bit.ly/315FZkR

"Political system." ScienceDaily. https://bit.ly/3G12yGm

"The road to democracy." The World's Children's Prize. https://bit.ly/3D4p3bC

"Trayvon Martin Shooting Fast Facts." *CNN*, February 17, 2021. https://cnn.it/3rgZMZG

Weinstein, Adam. "The Trayvon Martin Killing, Explained." Mother Jones, March 18, 2012. https://bit.ly/32KGYYD

"What Are Democratic Processes?" Human Rights Careers. https://bit.ly/3hKAfTA

Chapter 1

"America's Founding Documents." National Archives. www.archives.gov/founding-docs

Arana, Marie. "Latin Americans Are Souring on Democracy. That's Not So Surprising Considering the Region's History." *Time*, August 27, 2019. https://bit.ly/31e5xMQ

"Civil Rights Act of 1957." Dwight D. Eisenhower Presidential Library, Museum & Boyhood Home. https://bit.ly/3d6Zzjf

"Democracy Index 2020: In sickness and in health?" The Economist Intelligence Unit. https://bit.ly/3xyo1DT

"DR Congo country profile." *BBC News*. https://bbc.in/3rmoZSu

Emmanuel, Rachel. "Liberal MPs filibuster motion to review WE Charity payments to Trudeaus—again." *iPolitics*, October 9, 2020. bit.ly/3j0Pabw

"Explore Our Country, Our Parliament." Parliament of Canada. https://bit.ly/31bXJeL

"Global democracy has a very bad year." *The Economist*, February 2, 2021. https://econ.st/3FVLUrQ

"Law and the Rule of Law." Judicial Learning Center. https://bit.ly/3p7WZzn

Omar, Ilhan. "I Never Expected to See It Here." *The Atlantic*, January 21, 2021. https://bit.ly/3zGr2Se

Pilkington, Ed. "America's flawed democracy: the five key areas where it is failing." *The Guardian*, November 16, 2020. https://bit.ly/3iub5b4

"Presidential Election Process." USAGov. www.usa.gov/election

Shvili, Jason. "What Is Authoritarian Government?" World Atlas, March 25, 2021. https://bit.ly/3FYVt9y

"The Constitution." The White House. https://bit.ly/3pameB9

"The Racist Filibuster We Can't Afford to Forget." *The Takeaway*, August 29, 2016. bit.ly/3l3AATm

"The Rule of Law." LexisNexis. https://bit.ly/3o547gu

"Universal Declaration of Human Rights." United Nations. https://bit.ly/3roEYPV

"What Are Human Rights?" Canadian Human Rights Commission. www.chrc-ccdp.gc.ca/en/about-human-rights/what-are-human-rights

Chapter 2

"Colombia tax protests: At least 17 dead, ombudsman says." *BBC News*, May 3, 2021. https://bbc.in/32NY2wZ

Doerr, Audrey D. "Public Service." *The Canadian Encyclopedia*, December 16, 2013. https://bit.ly/316JQyC

"How Local Government Works." Association of Municipalities of Ontario. https://bit.ly/3o6drAA

"Introduction: The Democratic Process." Texas Gateway. https://bit.ly/3FS9ntU

"Knowing Your Roles: City and Town Governments Edition." Municipal Research and Services Center of Washington, January 21, 2020. https://bit.ly/3xRtxR4

Schaeffer, Katherine. "Racial, ethnic diversity increases yet again with the 117th Congress." *Pew Research Center*, January 28, 2021. pewrsr.ch/3xc9QCG

"State and Local Government." The White House. https://bit.ly/3D5LZqU

"The Abolishment of Jury System in Malaysia." ALSA National Chapter Malaysia. https://bit.ly/3E5Dw8J

Chapter 3

Barrow, Bill and Hilary Powell. "AP Interview: Stacey Abrams on voting rights, her next move." *AP News*, April 9, 2021. https://bit.ly/37366J0

Daley, Jim. "Killings By Police Declined After Black Lives Matter Protests." *Scientific American*, March 1, 2021. https://www.scientificamerican.com/article/killings-by-police-declined-after-black-lives-matter-protests1/

Drutman, Lee. "America Is Now the Divided Republic the Framers Feared." *The Atlantic*, January 2, 2020. https://bit.ly/3FYWmyU

King, Maya. "How Stacey Abrams and her band of believers turned Georgia blue." *Politico*, November 8, 2020. https://politi.co/3xAdzLQ

"What is Voter Suppression?" Anti-Defamation League. https://bit.ly/3cYuVsD

Chapter 4

Coletta, Amanda. "An unmarked gravesite drags a not-so-distant horror back into the spotlight. Is this a real reckoning?" *The Washington Post*, June 16, 2021. wapo.st/3xbHiJx

Harris, Kathleen. "Watchdog slams government's 'slow to non-existent' action to protect Canadians' privacy." *CBC News*, September 27, 2018. https://bit.ly/3xE3sWr

McDermott, Jackie. "Civic Virtue, and Why It Matters." National Constitution Center, February 20, 2020. constitutioncenter.org/blog/civic-virtue-and-why-it-matters

McKinley, Steve. "Until remains of 215 children found in Kamloops, two-thirds of Canadians say they knew just a little—or nothing—about residential schools." *Toronto Star*, June 15, 2021. https://bit.ly/3rHuUQf

National Centre for Truth and Reconciliation. nctr.ca

"Who We Are." Office of the Auditor General of Canada. www.oag-bvg.gc.ca/internet/English/au_fs_e_370.html

Glossary

activist A person who works to bring about social or political change

advocate A person who publicly supports a cause or policy

candidate A person nominated for election

censors Decides what parts of news stories are unacceptable and restricts people from seeing them

civic duty The responsibility of citizens, such as serving on a jury

Civil Rights Act Laws that prohibit the discrimination of people based on race, color, religion, sex, national origin, and other categories

deliberative process The process of thinking something through in order to make a judgement or form an opinion

gated community A walled community or place of residence that controls access

ground-penetrating radar Equipment that detects things underground

impartial Not biased, or treating all equally

indexes Ways to track performance

indifferent Having no preference or special interest

institutions Organizations or practices that exist within a society

juries Groups of people sworn to give a verdict in a court case

liberal democracy A set of political beliefs and a form of government that protects individual rights and freedoms

lobby To attempt to influence a government and sway it toward a desired goal

majority The greater number

minority Parts of a population differing from others in some way, such as ethnic origin

monarch A king or queen who is head of state

politicians People who are professionally involved in politics, or who are elected to office

polled Asked to give an opinion

protests Actions or statements aimed at expressing disapproval or objection to something

reconciliation The restoration of good or friendly relations between groups that have had disagreements, or where a party has been harmed

residential school A boarding school designed to assimilate Indigenous children

settlers People and their descendants, who have migrated to an area or colonized it to become permanent residents

suppression The act of keeping something from happening

unions Organizations of workers who come together for a common goal

Index

2021 Capitol Attack 18, 19

A
Abrams, Stacey 34
absolute monarchies 17
abuses of power 6, 14, 21, 23, 31, 38
accountability 5, 8, 11, 14, 21, 22, 24, 30, 38
American Revolution 15
autocracies 16, 17, 31

B
biases 30, 37, 43
Bill of Rights 9
Black Lives Matter movement 6, 14, 38
branches of government 22, 23, 24

C
Canada 5, 9, 11, 13, 20, 22, 23, 25, 26, 27, 33, 38, 40–41, 42
Canadian Charter of Rights and Freedoms 9
censoring 31
Chile 16
Civil Rights acts 13, 14
colonies 15
constitutions 7, 15, 16, 23, 36

D
Declaration of Independence 15

deliberative processes 5, 13, 39
democracy indexes 8
democratic processes 5, 12, 20, 25
discrimination 5, 6, 26, 43
diversity 22

E
elections 7, 8, 10, 11, 17, 18, 20, 21, 25, 32, 33, 34, 43

F
failed democracies 16, 42
filibusters 13
flawed democracies 8, 12, 16, 42
freedoms 5, 8, 9, 16, 17, 21, 27, 30, 31, 35, 37
full democracies 8, 9, 16

H
human rights 4, 5, 8, 9, 12, 13, 14, 15, 16, 17, 20, 21, 22, 24, 26, 28, 34, 36

I
Indigenous peoples 22, 36, 40–41, 43
inequalities 14, 37, 39, 43

J
jury duties 5, 20, 26

L
laws 5, 7, 13, 14, 23, 24, 27, 28, 29, 37, 39
liberal democracies 15, 27
liberties 9, 37
limiting powers 23
lobbying government 28, 29

M
majority rules 11, 12, 23, 39
March On Voting Rights 34
Martin, Trayvon 6
media 8, 27, 28, 30, 31, 35, 38, 39, 43
minorities 12, 34, 37, 39
monarchies 15, 17
municipal/local governments 22, 23, 25

P
parliaments 5, 12, 13, 23
participation 4, 9, 21, 36, 39, 42–43
petitioning 27, 39
political parties 7, 11, 13, 16, 20, 24, 32, 33, 35, 37, 42
political tolerance 12, 33, 37
presidents 6, 11, 18, 20, 22, 23, 34, 43
prime ministers 13, 20, 22, 23, 40
protesting 4, 6, 17, 18–19, 20, 27, 28, 34, 38, 39, 42

public service 20, 24, 28, 29, 38

R
ranking countries 8, 16
referendums 16, 21
representative democracies 4, 7
residential schools 40–41
rule of law 14, 27, 37, 39

S
special interest groups 28, 29, 35
student governments 4, 20

T
taxes 20, 25, 27, 28, 38, 39
threats to democracy 4, 12, 29, 31, 33

U
Universal Declaration of Human Rights 36

V
values 5, 6, 8, 9, 14, 16, 23, 31, 34, 35, 36, 43
voter supression 10, 33, 34

W
watchdogs 38

Y
youth 4, 6, 12, 32

About the Author

Rebecca Sjonger is the author of more than 50 non-fiction books for young people. She still remembers which candidate she voted for when she cast her first ballot almost 30 years ago!